Dredging

Sumpter Dredge No. 3 is the feature of Sumpter Valley Dredge State Park. Presently, the main activity of the park is for visitors to stop and look at the dredge. Eventually, visitors who camp at Union Creek Campground may be able to ride on the historic cars of the narrow gauge Sumpter Valley Railroad (restored) from the camp to the park, a distance of about 10 miles.

Monster Mantis Munches Mud, Gravel For Gold

Like some prehistoric monster, the Sumpter Valley Dredge gobbles up land, digests it to take out the gold then spews out the residue – rocks – that are dumped out the back of the dredger. Land is left in upside-down condition with the rocks on top, soil on the bottom.

Dredging For

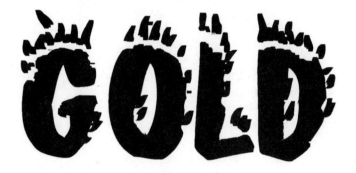

(Documentary)

Bert Webber

Webb Research Group Publishers

Published by
WEBB RESEARCH GROUP
Books About the Oregon Country
P. O. Box 314
Medford, Oregon 97501

Cover Pictures by Bert Webber
FRONT COVER: Sumpter Dredge No. 3 as presently seen in Sumpter Valley Dredge State Park at Sumpter, Oregon.
BACK COVER: Yuba Dredge No. 21 as presently seen in the Yuba Gold Field near Marysville, California.

Library of Congress Cataloging-in Publication Data

Dredging for gold : documentary / Bert Webber.
     p.   cm.
Includes bibliographical references and index.
ISBN 0-936738-83-9
1. Gold dredging—Oregon History. 2. Gold Dredging—Idaho—History.
3. Gold dredging—California—History. I. Title.
TN422.W43   1994   94-32075
622'. 342.2—dc20   CIP

Contents

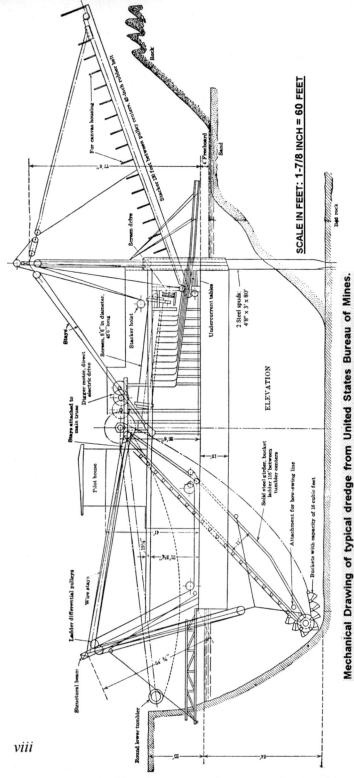

viii

Mechanical Drawing of typical dredge from United States Bureau of Mines. Dredges operated with as few as three men: the driver (winchman, pilot), fore and aft oilers. A well-maintained dredger worked 7 days a week, 24-hours a day but stopped about once a week for gold extraction and fixing.

SCALE IN FEET: 1-7/8 INCH = 60 FEET

For canvas housing

Stacker 126 feet between pulley centers. 48-inch rubber belt

Rock

Screen drive

Freeboard

Sand

Screen, 8'6" in diameter, 42'6" long

Stacker hoist

Undercurrent table

2 Steel spuds: 4'8" x 3' x 80'

Digger motor, direct electric drive

Stays attached to main truss

ELEVATION

Stays

Pilot house

Solid steel girder, bucket ladder 116 between tumbler centers

Bed rock

Ladder differential pulleys

Wire stays

Attachment for bow-swing line

Buckets with capacity of 16 cubic feet

Structural beam

Round lower tumbler

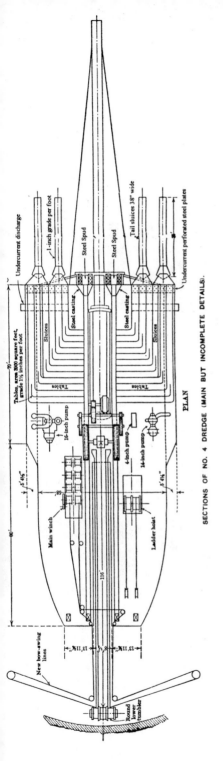

SECTIONS OF NO. 4 DREDGE (MAIN BUT INCOMPLETE DETAILS).

Dredge No. 4 (this drawing), was a Yuba and operated in the Yuba Gold Fields near Marysville, California. Although dredgers were very thorough in their operations, a dredge could glean gold from only as deep as its bucket-chain ladder would reach. Some fields were dredged several times, each time with a longer ladder. See Chapter 4 about the Dredge No. 21 operating in 1994.

Gold dredgers were invented in New Zealand. The first gold dredge in the United States (1894) operated near Bannock, Montana and it was named the *Fielding L. Graves* in 1895. Many visitors from New York, Chicago, and elsewhere attended the christening ceremony. Only a few dredges were named – most just had a number.

Introduction: What's a "Dredge"?

A gold dredge, also called a "dredger," is a weird looking apparatus that some say resembles a giant praying mantis that creaks, clatters, emits horrendous screams and groans as it digs rocks and sand from the bottom of a river or pond then, after digesting into its bowels what it seeks – gold – spews waste out its back side leaving acres of mountains of rocks.

While some call a dredge a Rube Goldberg* contrivance for panning gold, these dredges, often five stories tall and many of them well over 100 feet long, are the infinite way of obtaining even the slightest flakes of fine gold that stream-side panners could never capture.

> A gold dredge is a complicated system of engines and/or motors, winches, cables, part hydraulic-operated devices, sluice boxes with quicksilver recovery units, shaking jigs, water pumps, sand and water discharge plumbing, and a conveyor stacker that dumps rocky residue behind the dredge. A dredge does not waste fresh water for when a dredge needs to move, it moves its pond with it.

---

* Rube Goldberg, 1883-1970. U. S. cartoonist who comically thought up involved contrivances, often very complicated machines, to do a seemingly simple task.

A ladder dredge employs a continuous chain of buckets rotating around a rigid adjustable frame called a ladder. When the ladder is lowered, at a slant, to the bottom of a river or pond, the empty buckets descend along the underside of the ladder to the bottom where they dig into the mud. The loaded buckets return along the ladder's upper side and dumps its contents in a hopper at the top of the bucket-line's reach.

Long, heavy stakes, sometimes of wood but often of metal, called spuds, are frequently used to anchor a dredge to the bottom of a river or pond. A dredge can pivot on the spud to change angle in the water for reaching new digging sites. On some dredges, lengths of wire-rope tie the dredge to the bank for stability.

Gold is recovered by placer mining of sand and rock deposits and by lode or vein mining in mountainous terrain. Placer mining, the oldest method, entails the heaviness of gold to separate it from the much lighter material with which it is found. The deposits mined by the placer method are the gold-bearing sands and gravel that have been deposited by rapidly moving streams and rivers at places where these streams widen and lose speed. As the current slows, the sediment being carried down stream settles to the bottom.

Hydraulic mining came before dredges. In California (where hydraulic mining was invented), Oregon, Idaho and Montana, thick layers of gravel on hillsides were blasted by high-powered jets of water thereby crumbing the hills into swill which ran through long lines of sluice boxes. Gold nuggets and fine flakes were caught in the riffles in the boxes as the sand and gravel were carried over the top of the riffles.

This method of mining was profitable but required much water and a lot of land. The water was available for the taking. Usually the land was privately owned and had to be negotiated for. Sometimes many miles of flumes or pipes were needed to get the water to the hydraulic mining sites. Costs were minimal compared with the value of the gold recovered thus even the poorest of ground was suitable for hydraulic mining.

Records in county agencies provided values for farm and orchard acerages. These values were computed against the results from test drillings in those lands. In thousands of acres, the potential royalties to be paid a land owner from the gold to be mined far exceeded anything the agriculturist could ever expect to earn from his farming. Much of this land was leased, or purchased outright, by mining companies.

After hydraulic operations had been going for awhile, the sand, mud and rocks thrown out after the gold recovery washed on down the rivers as silt bringing such significant complaint from farmers and orchardists, that legislation against hydraulic mining became effective in 1881. Thereafter, at least in California, future blasting of hillsides by jets of water from hydraulic "Giant" and "Monitor" nozzles was very limited.

Hydraulic methods were sometimes used in conjunction with the dredgers to break down high banks confronting the dredges.

About the turn of the century, gold mining by use of dredges became the paramount method of placer mining. The principle of the gold dredge was based on experience with dredges used for deepening rivers and harbors for ships. The adaptation of the harbor dredge to gold mining was invented in New Zealand and quickly spread throughout the world.

While the first dredges (harbor and river improvement for ships) were often built on ship hulls, a new style of dredge emerged for digging for gold. These dredges, built on pontoons, could be used in a shallow river, creek or even from a pond well away from any source of free-flowing water. This became known as paddock dredging.

Dredges are known by a variety of terms: boats, vessels, barges being the most common. The paddock dredge merely floated in its own pond that is continuously extended by the digging equipment – the bucket line – attached to one end of a dredge. To the rear of the dredge, the pond fills in with the waste product – rocks – called "tailings," that emerge out the back of the dredge at the end of the gold recovery process. Accordingly, the dredge moves about taking its pond with it.

It would seem that the best ground for a dredge to work would be level ground but if the exploratory drilling of test holes to determine where the gold is located happened to be up-hill from the site then being worked, the dredge merely spews its discharged gravel in higher mounds around the pond thus elevating the water

13

The dredge "lost" in the underbrush near Sumpter is the drag-line end of a "doodle-bug" operation.
It is known as a MONIGAN or MONIGHAN.
One model built by Bucyrus was a MONICKER.

14

"Doodle-bug" working Johnson Placer Claim on Upper Pleasant Creek in Jackson County, Oregon. The year was 1960.

level. This method allows the dredger to continue uphill.

The number of dredges* working in the various western states at any one time varies widely depending on the source consulted. In 1904, there were 49 reported in California. By 1910, as many as 72 were counted in California alone. One source claims there were 60 in Idaho but there is no date established. Montana and Oregon appear to have had a lesser number. We have found one for certain in Washington.

Gold recovery by dredges is not confined to the United States (including Alaska). For decades dredges have operated throughout the world. For a list, please see the Appendix.

*   *   *

Several people were of special assistance in the preparation of this book and are acknowledged here with pleasure.

---

* Dredges referred to here are the large fully self-contained barges that were many times at least 100 feet long and about 50 feet wide. Small one or two-man operation "doodlebug" dredges are a variety sometimes 30 feet long that became common sights on small creeks. These are not counted here.

Bill Dobbyn, a placer miner of Jacksonville, Oregon, had a 30-foot long "doodle-bug" dredge that operated with a dragline in Jackson Creek at the Jacksonville city limits in the 1930's. He told us about this adventure for which we are appreciative.

Also in Oregon, James R. "Jim" Evans, Baker City, and Larry and Nancy Wilson, Clackamas and Sumpter, helped with details and photographs about the Sumpter Valley Dredge No. 3. We acknowledge the special assistance of Richard E. Webber, Stratford, NJ, who provided some of his photographs. Nancy Wilson also knew where the old "Monighan" "doodle-bug" was hidden in the weeds, near Sumpter, and went there to photograph it for this book. We appreciate the friendly suport of these folks.

The site and dredge, at Sumpter, Oregon where Sumpter Dredge No. 3 sits in its pond, has been purchased by the State of Oregon for a park. This park has been named Sumpter Valley Dredge State Park. Of special assistance was Kathy Schutt, Master Planning Team Leader, who provided an advance copy of the *Master Plan* for this new park. We thank Kathy for her interest and assistance.

With the help of several of the Reference Librarians at the Jackson County Library's Main Branch in Medford, we determined that Sumpter Dredge No. 3 was listed in the *National Register of Historic Places* (No. 71000676) as of Oct 26, 1971. No publically available sign or plaque about this has been found at the dredge as of this writing.

Richard "Dick" Portal, a valued colleague, who is a retired Reference Librarian, earlier of Medford now in Salem, went to the Oregon State Library and the Salem Public Library searching for esoteric matter on gold-digging dredges. His prowling in "old stuff" brought up numerous obscure but very pertinent writings some of which has been incorporated here. These are included in the bibliography. Dick, you are a gem!

We found what was left of Sumpter Dredge No. 2 near Liberty, Washington right where it quit work. For better identification of this 2nd-hand dredge, and its work in that location, we have dubbed it the "Liberty Dredge." We visited with a number of the folks in that village among whom are Ed Guse, Ralph Fackler and Wesley Engstrom. They told us exactly where to look for the

Ken McKenzie in pilot house of Yankee Fork Dredge in summer 1994. In 1940 he helped build this dredge. Art Packard (right) also worked on this dredge years ago. Visitors can tour the dredge in summer for a small fee.

identifiable remains. We acknowledge their friendly help.

In Idaho, we visited with Ken McKenzie and Art Packard. Ken, as a young man, helped build the Yankee Fork Dredge then later worked on it. Currently he is the chief interpreter and tour guide for the Yankee Fork Gold Dredge Association. He took us on a detailed inspection of the boat where we were able to photograph it, from top-to-bottom and stem-to-stern, for this project. Art, who worked on the dredge years ago is "Mr. Dredge" when it comes to the history of gold dredges. He also wrote the book, *Gold Dredge on the Yankee Fork* and has allowed us to quote from it. We acknowledge the friendly visits and assistance of these gentlemen.

Dave Sbaffi and June Hose talk about Yuba No. 21's operations during supervised visit to dredge in July 1994.

We appreciate the interest and assistance of June Hose of the Folsom Historical Museum, Folsom, and Julie Stark of the Community Memorial Museum in Yuba City, California. With June, we were invited to witness the giant Yuba No. 21 as it took a break from its 24-hour-a-day, nearly 7-days-a-week digging (and obtaining) gold near Marysville, California. We were privileged to meet Dave Sbaffi, General Manager of Cal Sierra Development, Inc., who made room in his schedule to take us on a guided tour of the Yuba No. 21 operation. Both of us are indebted to Dave for this first-hand lesson in this dredge's operations as well as for his interest and professional friendliness.

This work was not planned to be exhaustive about gold dredging, but is intended to entertain and instruct about how and where a few of these earth-disrupting monsters, that produced millions of dollars in gold for nearly a century, worked. What happened to all that gold? Some folks can look in a mirror at their teeth and will find some of it.

The author is sensible that there may be some typographical and other errors in the following work; but as they will be found *few* and *inconsiderable*, it is not worthwhile to notice them.

—borrowed from Estwick Evans (1819). Even so, constructive comments to the author are welcome and may be sent in care of the publisher whose address is on page *vi*.

Bert Webber
Central Point, Oregon

Chapter 1.
Sumpter's Dredges

The dredge on exhibit at Sumpter Valley Dredge State Park, Sumpter, Oregon, is the third of the species to be built and used in the Sumpter area. All three dredges are of the Yuba design. The first, called Sumpter No. 1, started digging its way downstream from the town where it had been built on January 7, 1913. It stopped on July 23, 1924. The bones of its hull are clearly visible, in the swamp, just a few feet north of the Dredge Station of the Sumper Valley Restoration Railroad. This is just south, by a few hundred yards, of the ghost town of McEwan on Highway 7. At this writing, there is no interpretative sign identifying these remains as being what's left of this dredge.

Sumpter No. 2, also constructed at Sumpter, operated between October 1915 and 1923 and worked upstream from where it was assembled. Just beyond town, it went up Cracker Creek in the direction of Bourne. After its operation shut down, No. 2 was dismantled, except for the hull, and its parts were moved to Central Washington. The operation there is in the Chapter 2, "Liberty Dredge on Swauk Creek."

The No. 3 Dredge, the feature of the Oregon State Park at Sumpter, was built in 1935 using many of the parts salvaged from Sumpter No. 1. The usual way of site preparation for building a dredge was to scoop out a large pit then build the hull in the pit. When construction was completed, water would be turned into the pit therefore floating the hull. Once afloat, the machinery would be installed. When ready for work, the dredge started digging right where it was.

Sumpter No. 3, however, was built like a ship, on ways, on the bank of the pond. When the hull and basic frame was ready, the pins were pulled and the hull splashed into the water. The hull launching was on April 16, 1935 amid much celebration. With all the machinery finally in place, No. 3 was ready to dig by June 26th of the same year.

Sumpter Dredge No. 3 is the center-piece of the Sumpter Valley Dredge State Park. Present buildings are destined for replacement. Plans call for Sumpter Valley Restoration Railroad to extend its track to encircle the dredge.

Considering that No. 1 stopped work in 1924 and was idle for over a decade, the happening that spurred new life into gold mining was an increase in the price paid for gold by the federal government. In earlier years, $20 per Troy ounce was the set price. In 1934, the President of the United states, Franklin Delano Roosevelt, raised the price to $35.00 per ounce. Accordingly, a new era started for gold prospectors.

It was good times in the gold mining business for the next eight years. Not only did the old hard-rock mines become active,

SUMPTER VALLEY GOLD DREDGE

EST. 1935

Began operating 1935. Closed August 1954.
Employing 23, dredging was done 24 hrs. daily
except July 4th and Christmas.
The 72, 1 ton, 9 cu. ft. buckets dumped 25 buckets/min. for
average production of 280,000 cu. yds. per month.
The 250 hp. bucket line motor powered by 12 mi., 23,000 volt
electric line from a portable substation.
3000 gpm of water supplied by (2) 10 in. & (1) 6 in. pumps with
(6) 24 in. American jigs & sluice boxes for gold recovery.
Boat hull measures 52 × 120 × 11 ft., stacker is 96 ft. long.
Dredge cost $300,000 and produced $4.5 Million in gold.

←LEFT PAGE - **Buckets on Sumpter Dredge No. 3.**
THIS PAGE - **The gantry and bucket chain.**

but many of the dredges throughout the western United States were cleaned up and started digging again.

In October of 1942, nearly a year after the start of World War II, – the "day that will live in infamy," the Japanese attack on Pearl Harbor – non-essential mining (which included gold mining) was ordered halted for the duration of the war. The machinery, especially wire rope, required for gold mining, was essential for critical war industry.

With the surrender of Germany in May 1945, and the issue in the war against Japan highly favoring the allies, the War Production Board declared that gold mining could resume as of July 5,

Starboard stern of dredger. Water, from the pond used in processing, was discharged back into the pond from the troughs.

1945. (Japan capitulated on August 15.) Sumpter No. 3 was dusted off, its systems were checked and it went back into business until final shutdown in 1954. It is viewed today right where it quit work.

*   *   *

Some Operational Matters

During its life as an operating dredger, Dredge No. 3 had three owners. These were The Sumpter Valley Dredging Company, the Baker Dredging Company and the Powder River Dredging Company.

How much money did the miners earn for all this work? Many, including major firms, wouldn't talk. The U. S. Mint issued reports to each miner who either bragged about his achievement or kept his mouth shut. At intervals, the mint reported publicly the value of gold that came in from the miners but

Sumpter Dredge No. 3 as it appeared on June 15, 1994. The pond is unofficially called "Reflection Pond" for when one thinks back over the history of dredging in the valley, as well as for the reflection of the dredge in the pond on a late summer afternoon. Until the dredge can be refurbished as the feature of the Sumpter Valley Dredge State Park, the broken windows have been patched with sheets of particle board.

never revealed how much money went to individual operations. It does not appear that in those days there was any cross-checking between the mint and the income-tax "snoops" as the Internal Revenue Service was often called.*

Some reports are these:

At the close of a 6-year operation in Eastern Oregon, a dredge operator reported a gross of $500,000.

It has been said but never documented that all three of the Sumpter dredgers, including the several doodle-bugs, plausibly recovered about $10 million in gross receipts. This was primarily gold but other metals are generally found on assay.

For Sumpter No. 3, with a daily operating cost of about $700, to show a reasonable profit the gold recovery would need to be about $1,000 each day. ☐

---

* Some placer miners working the streams on weekends today indicate they peddle their unrefined gold to private jewelry makers or to other buyers and snicker at any mention that the IRS knows about it. There are a few rural stores that maintain old fashioned gold scales and accept gold dust in trade to the present time.

Rick Webber photographs the dredge from the new path built recently all the way around the dredge. He is outside the new safety fence.

Getting to Sumpter Valley Dredge State Park

The park is on the edge of the town of Sumpter on the left of Highway 220 as one enters the village from Highway 7. Sumpter is at 4,480-ft. elev. It is listed as 27 miles west of Baker City.   —Editor

According to the *Master Plan* for Sumpter Valley Dredge State Park, it is envisioned that the Sumpter Valley Restoration Railroad will extend its track to encircle the dredge and add an additional station at the dredge.

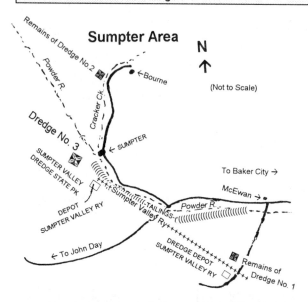

Sumpter Dredge No. 2. The timber on the land had to be felled then stumps pulled before the dredge could operate.

Specifications of the Sumpter Dredgers:

Sumpter Dredge No. 1

Construction design: Yuba
Hull length: 100 feet
Hull beam: 45 feet
Buckets: 65
Maximum dig depth: 30 feet
Bucket size: 9 cu. ft.
Rate of speed, 21 buckets per minute
Estimated area dug in 1 year: 60 acres
Trommel: ¾-inch flow-through holes
Gantry construction of timber
Hull: wood
Superstructure: wood
Operating power: Electric (Eastern Oregon Light & Power Co.)
Heating system for winter operation: cord wood to fire boiler
Winch room and stacker (rear oiler room) heat: oil stoves
Recovery method: sluices with riffles
Disposition: Dismantled, with many parts installed on Sumpter Dredge
No. 3. Remains of hull seen in swamp near Dredge Depot of
Sumpter Valley Restoration Railroad.

Sumpter Dredge No. 2

Construction design: Yuba
Hull length: 100 feet
Hull beam: 45 feet
Buckets: 65
Pumps: 2 @ 10-inch and 1 @ 6-inch (8,000 gal. min.)
Maximum dig depth: 30 feet

27

Bucket size: 7½ cu. ft.
Rate of speed, 21 buckets per minute
Estimated area dug in 1 year: 60 acres
Trommel: 6 x 36-feet with ¾-inch flow-through holes
Gantry construction of timber
Hull: wood
Superstructure: sheet steel
Operating power: Electric (Eastern Oregon Light & Power Co. – 12-miles)
Heating system for winter operation: oil fired boiler
Winch room and stacker (rear oiler room) heat : oil stoves
Recovery method: sluices, 42,000 sq. ft. with riffles plus SAVE-ALL
Disposition: Dismantled except hull. Equipment freighted to Liberty,
       Washington where it worked until confronted by bank of hard
       rock. Dismantled for parts. Hull, in pond, remains. Photo page 37.

Sumpter Dredge No. 3

Construction design: Yuba
Hull length 125 feet
Hull beam: 52 feet
Buckets: 72
Bucket size: 9 cu. ft.
Rate of speed, 25 buckets per minute
Estimated area dug in 1 year: 100 acres.
Gantry construction of structural steel
Operating power: electric
Recovery method: sluices until post WW-II then jigs
Stacker: 96-feet with 35-inch discharge belt
Disposition: Some machinery removed and sold. Super-structure, bucket
       ladder, stacker are intact. This dredge is the centerpiece of
       Sumpter Valley Dredge State Park, Sumpter, Oregon.

Tailings from the dredgers as viewed from the south. The light-colored object directly beneath the mountain peak is the stacker on the dredge. In foreground is swamp area near the Powder River.

Remains of hull from Dredge No. 2 on the road between Sumpter and Bourne. Note tailings in rear.

LOWER↓ Small size commercial gold rocker, along with pan, one might use on a weekend of prospecting. It is wise to consult as to land ownership for permission to pan, as many streams have legal mining claims staked on them.

The 1915 model Heisler geared logging locomotive that worked on the original Sumpter Valley Railroad, now hauls passengers in antique cars on summer weekends. RIGHT: Track was relocated on top of tailings to allow the dredge to dig under the original right-of-way. LOWER: Straight line in tailings is the relocated railroad.

30

Remains of Dredge No. 1 rot in swamp next to the Dredge Depot of the SVR.

S.V.R. DREDGE DEPOT

Calm and serene Olive Lake, which fed water through penstock tube to the power house of the Fremont Power Plant. (Photographed spring 1993) Electricity from here operated all three Sumpter dredges.

Reconditioned trommel offered for sale ($8,900) at Sumpter in June 1994. Rick Webber stands at hopper (TOP) and at bottom where the tailings emerge.

33

It was a time for reminiscing for those former workers on the dredge, who could be located, when they gathered at Sumpter for picnic and reunion on June 12, 1994.

From left to right (by numbers):

1. Larry Graves
2. Hank Potts
3. Bud Howard
4. George Hansen
5. Charlisle Woodley - Drill team
6. Jim Ego - Electrician
7. Ralph Allen - Superintendent - jig; Dredge Master - engineer
8. Albert Langlitz
9. Wilson Dickison - Oiler
10. Ted Hixson
11. Jim Kinkaid - Electrician
12. Rod Dickison

Certificate of Membership

WILSON DICKISON

is a

1994 Gold Card HONORARY LIFE
Member of the

Friends of the Sumpter Valley Dredge

Ray Maher, President   Raul Racey, Treasurer   Jerry Myers, Bd. Member
Kent Bailey, Vice-President Richard Langrell, Bd. Member
Venita Cullom, Secretary   Bea Ice, Bd. Member

Wilson Dickison, one of the former dredgers, displays the certificate awarded to him, and the others, at the get-together at Sumpter on June 12, 1994.

35

Sumpter Dredge No. 2, renamed Liberty Dredge, shown in final resting pond near Liberty, Washington on July 16, 1994. LOWER: As viewed when working probably no later than 1928.

Chapter 2.
Liberty Dredge on Swauk Creek

The 2nd-hand Sumpter Dredge No. 2 was set up on Williams Creek in the vicinity of the ghost towns of Meaghersville and what is called Old Liberty. These sites are just off the Blewett Pass Highway No. 97, a short distance north of Ellensburg near the turnoff to present village of Liberty. These places are in Central Washington state. Clearly visible at this writing, the only remains are timbers from the collapsed super-structure and the hull. Ralph Fackler, now in his senior years, vividly recalls using the hull as a diving platform for swimming.

Frank Bryant, a former mineral examiner for the United States Department of the Interior, arrived in the Liberty area near where Williams and Swauk Creek meet in Kittitas County. It was 1925. He was on proven gold-bearing ground and was able to influence many wealthy people in buying stock in what became the Swauk Mining and Dredging Company. Some years earlier he had run a small gasoline powered dredge fitted with 2 cu. ft. buckets. He did very well but he needed a bigger dredge. Learning that Sumpter No., 2 was idle and for sale, he bought it. Jordan wrote:

Eighteen railroad cars were needed to help transport the dredge which had a 350 horsepower motor. On February 22, 1926, the dredge began its first operation [as] hundreds of people spent Washington's Birthday watching the big dredge swing into action for the first time. Forty people came from Seattle on a special sleeper [train] the preceding evening. Typical of Bryant's showmanship was an American Flag floating high over the dredge. The dredge worked three hours that day with crowds watching, newspapermen questioning and a movie camera grinding. *

---

* The "movie camera grinding" undoubtedly refers to Will E. Hudson, field cameraman in the Pacific Northwest who shot news and feature stories for Pathe Newsreel. Hudson worked out of Seattle and was the first newsreel cameraman in the area dating from 1912.

The mining firm never made any statements as to how much gold was recovered but a newspaperman said there was at least $50,000 worth but he didn't say in what time period.

There was another big party the following March when on the 15th, a special Pullman sleeper railroad car from Seattle brought visitors that swelled the crowds to about 2,000 people. Many of these folks, former placer miners in Alaska, had brought their pans with them and took turns bringing up "colors" from the stream.

A report in a house paper, the *Puget Sound Electric Journal*, by E. A. Batwell, quoted by Jordan reveals:

Gravels of different coarseness are screened through the rumble [*sic.-trommel*] and to the riffles where the gold makes its first acquaintance with mercury. From the riffles the gold impregnates the quicksilver and is taken to the amalgamator house where the mass is processed. From the amalgamator the gold bearing mercury is taken and the steel plates are carefully scraped of everything that has the appearance of value and is put into the container or the crucible. When the heat is applied, the mercury is driven off in the way of vapor and through a condenser pipe into an enameled pan of water where the mercury solidifies and is ready to on its way again separating gold from foreign matter.

At the end of this separation process, the molten gold was poured into molds making bricks that weighed about twelve pounds.

Swauk Creek, which fairly well parallels present Blewett Pass Highway, does not have very deep water and the gravel, where the gold is deposited, is fairly close to bed rock. Because of these factors, the dredge was really too big to work there. Accordingly, the entire operation – including the Liberty Dredge – was transported into nearby Deer Gulch. The gulch was known to be gold-bearing and Bryant had a hardrock mine about 100 feet away from the dredge site.

The dredge worked in its own pond at the new place for only 71 days then it was confronted with a 200 foot bank of heavy rock. An article appeared in the *Evening Record* at Ellensburg:

The Kittitas Gold Mining Co. ... was officered and managed by highly respected, well known and successful Northwest businessmen. These men were not essentially mining men and a wide divergence of opinion as to how the ground shouild be dredged arose at times, with the inmevitable result that no really definite policy or definite objective was ever fully outlined. Furthermore, it became evident that although the dredge could dig and wash a 65-foot bank, it could not [no longer] stack its tailings [as] no money was available to lengthen the stacker as all stock had been withdrawn from sale.

Jordan concluded that Liberty Dredge was way too big to work in Swauk Creek and much too small to properly work the over-burdon found at Williams Creek. The paper reported:

So the operation folded up and Frank Bryan became the scapegoat for all the problems of the company. Many of the stockholders looked on him as a fraud.

Bryant continued to occupy his campsite adjacent from the dredge which, as we have seen, was also just a stone's throw from his hardrock mine.* □

Getting to Liberty Dredge

Follow Highway 97 north from Ellensburg to the junction marked "Liberty" on the east (right) side of the road just beyond the concrete bridge. Back-track at the bridge noticing a narrow dirt road at the south end of the bridge, but proceed to the 2nd dirt (unimproved) road, also on the east side of highway. Proceed up a steep hill about ¼ mile and park near sheet-iron shack. Hike about 100 feet north to the pond and the remains of the Liberty Dredge. Site is 2,673 ft. elevation.   —Editor

Liberty Area

N ↑

Swauk Creek

Highway No. 97

Liberty →

Local High way

BRIDGE →

← Williams Creek

☒ ← Liberty Dredge

← CLE ELUM   ELLENSBURG →

(Not to scale)

---

* The author's field trip to Liberty was shared by son Dale Webber and one of his sons, Jason, 10. After admiring the Liberty Dredge and photographing it from all available angles, we discovered what is believed to have been Frank Bryant's mine shaft and tunnel into his mine. It seems well braced against intruders.

Chapter 3.
The Dredge on the Yankee Fork

The Yankee Fork of the Salmon River penetrates an area of Central Idaho noted for big game, great fishing, high-elevation camping and in years past, lots of gold. The ghost towns of Custer and Bonanza, alongside the river, were once thriving metropolises.

In 1939, the Snake River Mining Company drilled test holes along the Yankee Fork to see if dredging the river for gold was feasible. An earlier plan for dredging (1932) came to nothing after it was discovered that the 3 cu. ft. buckets, on a Yuba dredge,

The reconditioned Bucyrus-Erie dredge near Custer, Idaho that is open to visitors in summers. RIGHT: Its bucket line.

were too small to properly work in the hard packed gravel and fairly large size boulders found there. That dredge was moved to another site where the going would be easier.

More test drilling was done on a carefully marked grid of the area. After panning the core samples, it was estimated there was as much as $11 million in gold waiting to be dug. The investors decided to name their enterprise The Snake River Mining

TOP: Dredgemaster's view of bucket line from pilot house. When an exceptionally large boulder came up, he could throw a lever and dump it out a trap door. LOWER: The pristine Yankee Fork of the Salmon River near village of Sunbeam.

Manufacturer's bronze name plate in pilot house. Dredge weighs 988.125 tons. Is designated as Type: Self-Powered, floating bucketline, California

Company, although the Snake was nowhere near the Yankee Fork of the Salmon River.

The Yuba Manufacturing Company had visited the site for the earlier project so when an invitation to bid on the new dredge was circulated, Yuba did not appear. Bucyrus-Erie Company won the contract for a 988 ton dredge on January 15, 1940. Obviously stronger buckets were required so B-E agreed to build them. The huge dredge had a huge price: $309,968.

One of the features of the design called for a way for the dredge-master to view the contents of the buckets as they came up the ladder. When an exceptionally large rock had been bucketed, with the push of a lever he could hydraulically operate a chute that opened and dumped the boulder out the side of the dredge. This, instead of allowing the big rock to smash the upper hopper into which it, with the smaller rocks, gravel and river-bottom sand (and gold!) were washed with water under pressure.

Nearly all dredge operations worked around the clock therefore, when coming upon a dredge at night, one views a four-to-five story tall; "building" that not only emits all of those strange sounds, but resembles a huge cruise ship, or a four-story hotel, in the midst, of the mountains, because of all of its lights.

The Yankee Fork Dredge was assembled where it would start working. Art Packard wrote:

45

The job of trucking the dredge [parts] into the Yankee Fork Valley was a spectacular feat. Over 60 loads of huge pontoons and heavy structural steel made the climb over the Galena Summit with its narrow, twisting road and rickety bridges, grossly overworking the small, inadequate trucks of the thirties. Only one major mishap occurred in which a loaded pontoon turned over on its side on a narrow switchback.

The really heavy materials came from Bucyrus-Erie to the railhead at McKey. There, the Lindburg Trucking Company managed to unload the gigantic machinery from the rail cars onto their trucks with just pry-bars, jacks and strong backs. Their heavy Diamond-T truck, brought in such loads as the 17½ ton spud and huge swing winches through the narrow Spar Canyon Road.

Although great care was taken in moving every piece of equipment, every nut-and-bolt to the Yankee Fork, Packard found one incident of misfortune. The Lindburg's were misinformed as to the weight of the lower tumbler so when it was unloaded from the railroad car, it landed on the Ford truck with such a thud that the truck bed was "smashed to the ground levering the nose of the truck straight up in the air."

Huge spuds being hauled to dredge construction sites. Note early day trucking equipment. Locations, dates, unknown.

46

Yankee Creek Dredge is on Forest Service Road north of Sunbeam.
INSET: **Example of stacker in dumping rocks. (Yuba Gold Field).**

It was just 116 days from the start of assembly on April 1, until August 24th, when the Ingersoll-Rand diesels were fired for the first time on trial "for twenty minutes."

Operations

When the dredge was ready for work, the position-stabilizing spud and the bucketline were hoisted clear then the dredger was

Original rubber conveyor belt in stacker and one of many rollers. The fork-like device is a tilt-guard. The guard would tilt to pass a large out-bound rock, but the guard stopped the rock should it roll backwards.

TOP: Two, 450 HP Ingersoll-Rand 7-cyl. 12-inch bore diesel engines – one shown– (delivered 375 HP at 6,000 ft elev.) drove 243KVA electric generators to power dredge. Fuel tanks stored 18,350 gals oil – burned 600 gals/day. The engines weigh 81,250 lbs. LOWER: Ken McKenzie, who helped build dredge in 1940, is, in 1994, volunteer tour leader.

Heavy winches hold wire rope (cable) to operate bucket ladder and swing the dredge to new digging positions. Ladder hoist TOP was double drum with automatic brake powered by 100 HP motor. Swing-winch was 6-drums (5 shown) with 40 HP motor.

located where it was to start work. Wire rope lines were passed ashore and tied down when the bucket chain was hovering over the bank about 10 feet from the edge of the pond. First, the spud was lowered to the bottom of the water well where it became a pivot around which the dredge might arc back-and-forth digging

50

Bull gear is 12-ft diameter, came in 2 sections as seen below.

One of two speed controllers, this for bow and stern cables.

constantly, always lowering the buckets until the buckets reached bed rock. The ladder, 85 feet long, could dig as much as 37 feet below the surface of the pond. After the bottom of the dig, the dredge was swung left or right, as the case might be. When it came time to "step ahead," the spud was lifted and the slack taken up on the wire rope first on the port then on the starboard side "waddling" the dredger ahead a few feet.

(On those dredges with two spuds, the dredge walked ahead pivoting first on one then on the other. On these dual-spud machines, the main anchoring spud was of steel while the secondary spud was of wood. These spuds were huge being 50 to 70 feet long and of 35,000 to 50,000 pounds weight.)

On the Yankee Fork Dredge, the buckets were over 1-ton each (empty). As there were 71 buckets, the total weight suspended over the bow of the dredge was tremendous, which accounts for the need for the hefty Bucyrus-Eire gantry from which the bucketline was suspended. A counter-balance for the weight on the front of the dredge was the weighty stacker that carried the spoils – rocks – out the back end.

Extracting the gold on this dredge was done mainly by washing the gravel, mud and sand through a revolving screen

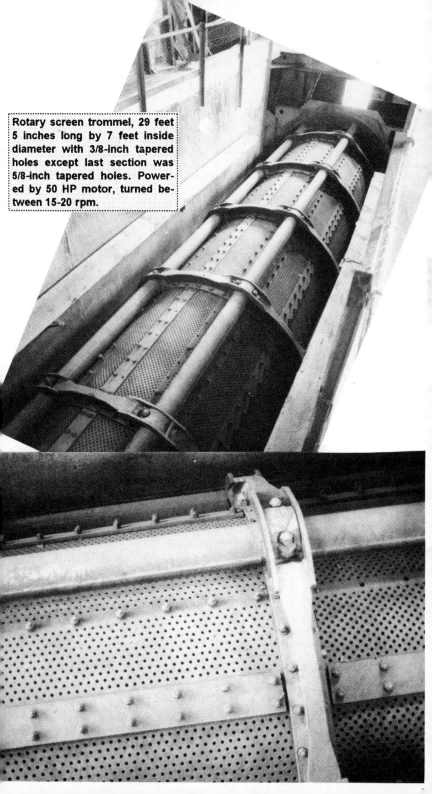

Rotary screen trommel, 29 feet 5 inches long by 7 feet inside diameter with 3/8-inch tapered holes except last section was 5/8-inch tapered holes. Powered by 50 HP motor, turned between 15-20 rpm.

Tailings in the Yankee Fork Valley opposite dredge. LOWER: Sign posted near Sunbeam provides sketch of history of the operation for visitors.

The roar of the engines, clatter of ladder and dumping of gravel was so noisy one's voice could not he heard therefore buzzer signals were used.

1 long 1 short = step ahead   1 long = stop

2 long = start   3 long = bow oiler to winch room

4 long = stern oiler to winch room   1 extra long = BIG ROCK COMING

5 short = bow oiler to front deck

YANKEE FORK DREDGE

THE SOIL DISTURBANCE VISABLE FROM THIS POINT AND CONTINUING FOR SIX MILES UP STREAM WAS CREATED BY A DREDGING OPERATION, WHICH STARTED IN OCTOBER OF 1939 AND CONTINUED UNTIL NOVEMBER OF 1942. OPERATION WAS DIS-CONTINUED DURING WORLD WAR II AND RESUMED AGAIN IN 1944. THE DREDGE WORKED APPROXIMATELY 10 MONTHS EACH YEAR UNTIL 1952.

THE DREDGE BUCKET LINE HAD SEVENTY TWO EIGHT CUBIC FOOT BUCKETS AND COULD DIG TO A DEPTH OF 35 FEET. ELEVEN FEET OF WATER WAS REQUIRED TO FLOAT THE DREDGE. INITIAL TESTS OF THE PLACER GROUND SHOWED THAT THERE WOULD BE APPROXIMATELY ELEVEN MILLION DOLLARS IN GOLD TO BE TAKEN FROM THE PATENTED MINING CLAIMS.

54

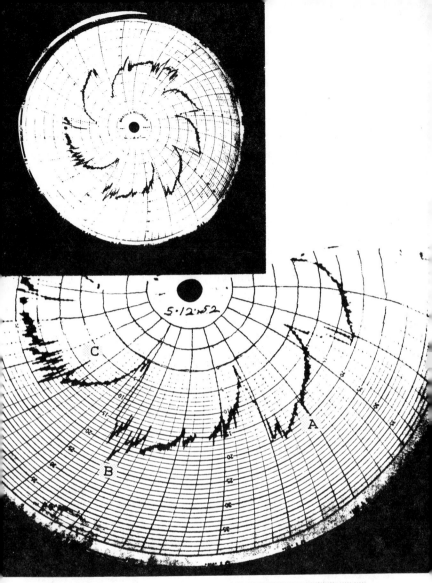

Electric clock on pilot house wall with pen drew performance of the dredge. Recorded time of day in 15 minute intervals and depth of the dig. If ladder was hoisted out of water this was shown. Examples from chart of May 12, 1952:

A - Digging at 19.5 feet at 4 pm

B - Digging at 24.5 feet at 8:14 pm

C - Digging at 8 feet at 10:22 pm

55

(trommel) 29-feet 5-inches long installed on a slight angle. This screen has an outside diameter of about 7-feet and turns while constant jets of water play on the goods dredged from the bottom of the pond. The trommel had 3/8ths-inch taperered holes through which water and all fine matter –gold and sand – passed. Then the gravel was spun out the stern end of the trommel onto the 105-foot long stacker's 42-inch wide curved conveyer belt at the end of which the gravel was systematically dumped in piles.

The slurry of mud and sand, with gold, and water, went into the 16, 20-foot long by 20-inchs wide sluice troughs on each side over riffles, the lower end being special mercury-containing copper plates. The total gold recovery area of these sluices was 1,066.6 sq.ft. With this capacity, the dredge could run for about two weeks between shut-downs for the "clean up."

> *Encyclopædia Britannica* in its **Eleventh Edition (1910) declares: "The sluice is considered to be the best contrivance for washing gold gravels." Most dredges used riffled sluices. Yuba No. 21, over 70 years later, uses a series of four jigs. See Chapter 4.**

Every living soul within at least a quarter-of-a-mile knew when clean up started for the great Ingersoll-Rand diesels fell silent and the creeking and banging of the buckets quieted. The riffles in the sluice troughs are carefully removed and water-washed with all the caked wet sand flowing forced to flow into the jig.

The "jig" is a hopper that contains metal shot. A small motor vibrates the jig where the final recovery of gold is separated from the sand and water which flows back into the pond. After mercury is added, it and the gold becomes gold amalgam. In some dredges, there is a stove on which the crucible of gold amalgam is placed and "cooked" at about 700 degrees F. The mercury is recovered by distillation and the molten gold remains in the pot. The final act is to pour the gold into molds formed about the size of a brick.

Most dredger outfits have a shack or other building a short distance from the dredge where the gold amalgam is melted and the mercury recovered. □

YANKEE FORK DREDGE SPECIFICATIONS*

Construction design: Bucyrus-Erie
Hull length 112.5 feet
Hull beam: 54 feet
Buckets: 72
Bucket size: 8 cu. ft.
Rate of speed, 26 buckets per minute
Gantry construction of structural steel
Operating power: Ingersoll-Rand 7 cylinder Diesel engines (2) w/electric drive
Recovery method: sluices, 16 on each side (total 32)
Stacker: 90-feet with 42-inch rubber discharge belt
Disposition: Preserved and reconditioned for visitors but some parts vandalized or missing.

---

* This is a summary. For a detailed list see *Gold Dredge on the Yankee Fork*.

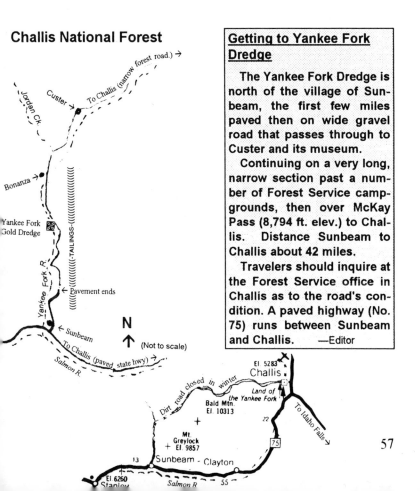

Challis National Forest

Getting to Yankee Fork Dredge

The Yankee Fork Dredge is north of the village of Sunbeam, the first few miles paved then on wide gravel road that passes through to Custer and its museum.

Continuing on a very long, narrow section past a number of Forest Service campgrounds, then over McKay Pass (8,794 ft. elev.) to Challis. Distance Sunbeam to Challis about 42 miles.

Travelers should inquire at the Forest Service office in Challis as to the road's condition. A paved highway (No. 75) runs between Sunbeam and Challis. —Editor

Yuba Dredge No. 21 works 24 hours a day, 7 days a week on private property in Yuba Gold Field east of Marysville, California. Photographed July 6, 1994.

Chapter 4.
The Yuba Gold Field
Mining by Cal Sierra Development, Inc.
as of December 18, 1992

The Yuba gold field is located about
50 miles north of Sacramento, California. There, the Yuba River emerges
from a gold bearing region of the Sierra
Nevada, exiting from steep, narrow can-
yons to flow onto the flood plain of the
Sacramento Valley. The material worn
from the mountains for millions of years
has dropped in the slower moving valley
stream bed to be washed and rewashed,
concentrating the gold.

A Dredge Named *Lisa*

Yuba Dredge No. 21 has had two sets of specifications. One set was for the dredge before World War II, when it was operated by Yuba Industries near Marysville, California, until it shut down in spring of 1968. The other specification came about in 1980-1981 when it was rebuilt and modernized for the present operations. (Chapter 4)

In the earlier period, this dredger was named *Lisa*. It had 110 buckets, each bucket with capacity of 18 cubic feet dumping 22 buckets per minute operated by two 500 HP motors. The maximum dig depth was 125 feet but more common was about 107 feet.

This dredge could easily dig about 100,000 cubic yards in a week.

The trommel screen was 9 feet by 55 feet with a stacker of 225 feet length. The tailings were about 12 miles long and 1½ miles wide this being about 11,000 acres.

Dredging for gold was commenced in the gold field by W. C. Hammon in 1904, with wooden hulled bucketline dredges, which dug to 16 feet below water level. The Yuba company shortly thereafter formed its own subsidiary for making dredges, at first in Marysville, then later in Benicia near Vallejo. By the 1930's there were 12 dredges operating at one time in the gold fields and by 1968, 21 dredges had been built and operated on the property. By 1968, more than one billion cubic yards of gravel had been mined for more than 5 million ounces of gold, worth about $140 million dollars when the gold was mined.

In 1968, a period of difficulty began because of the fixed gold price and steadily rising costs. Although an area of deep ore reserves was recognized, the price of gold was too low to justify the construction of the new machines required to mine to the depth of the reserve. By late 1976, Dredge No. 21, which had operated fitfully, was finally put on a care and maintenance basis.

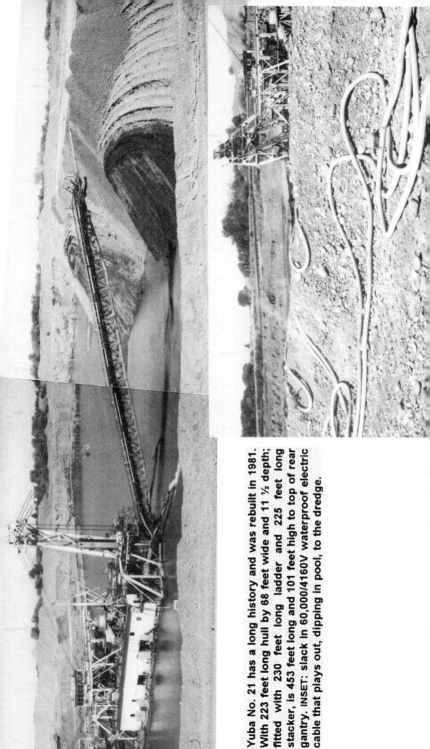

Yuba No. 21 has a long history and was rebuilt in 1981. With 223 feet long hull by 68 feet wide and 11 ½ feet depth; fitted with 230 feet long ladder and 225 feet long stacker, is 453 feet long and 101 feet high to top of rear gantry. INSET: slack in 60,000/4160V waterproof electric cable that plays out, dipping in pool, to the dredge.

61

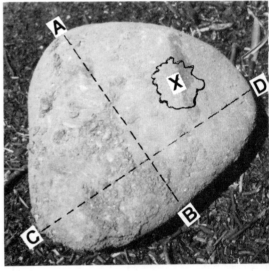

Every step one takes here is on tailings. Tailings from this operation are consigned to an aggregate company that makes little rocks (gravel) out of big rocks.

LOWER: Typical rock from tailings. This example weighs 4.75 lbs., is 5½-inches from A - B and 6 ½-inches from C - D. At X, is approx. 2¼-inches thick.

In 1979, a joint venture was formed between Yuba Consolidated Goldfields (then called Yuba Natural Resources), the owners of the property, and Placer Service Corp. (formerly called Yuba WestGold) to mine the deep reserve area. Dredge No. 21 was moved to the deep reserve and modified during 1980 and 1981. Mining operations commenced on October 1, 1981.

Before any of the present land could be dug, all the tailings from earlier dredgers had to be scrapped off by bulldozers.

The dredge has been rebuilt and presently has
> an extended bow gantry
> a longer digging ladder
> a new bucketline
> a more efficient main drive system
> a new electrical system conforming to OSHA/MSHA specifications
> a new hydraulic control system and control room
> a new gold saving plant and other modifications

Dredge No. 21 can now dig 140 feet below water level and is one of the deepest digging gold dredges in the world.*

Cal Sierra Development, Inc. (a wholly owned subsidiary of Robinson Enterprises, Inc.) purchased Dredge No. 21, all support assets and precious metals and mining rights on December 18, 1992.

Geology of the Cal Sierra Gold Fields

The occurrence of the Yuba River placer gold deposit is the result of a complex series of geological events. The original gravels were deposited by river systems during Eocene time in a

---

* On July 6, 1994, the water level of the pond in which Dredge No. 21 operates, was 48 feet below the level of the surrounding terrain. To keep the water level constant, pumps are used to draw off water that seeps into the pond. At this level, plus the 140 feet digging depth of the bucket line, gravel being dredged can be as much as 187 feet below the level of the surrounding land.

Stern of Yuba No. 21 showing water being expelled from dredge.

> Cal Sierra makes every effort to be a good neighbor, and contributes to the local economy. We strive to be environmentally sensitive. Our onboard recovery system is 100% gravity separation with no chemicals used. Dredge No. 21's power source is 100% environmentally acceptable electricity purchased from PG&E. We mine under an approved reclamation plan, stressing to leave the mined area in an improved state.
>
> —Dave Sbaffi, General Manager

tropical or near-tropical environment in which chemical decay predominated. Consequently, the rocks of these original gravels are primarily chemically resistant quartz from the original gold-quartz veins.

The original gravels were then covered by fragmented volcanic materials thrown onto the surface during Miocene and Pliocene time. During and immediately following the middle Tertiary volcanic activity, new stream systems developed and reworked and redeposited material of both prevolcanic and intervolcanic origin. In many instances, the reworking of the original gravels with large quantities of volcanic material resulted in deposits which are too low in grade to be economical.

After the late Tertiary volcanic activity, stream systems developed which eroded still deeper the load deposits formed in Upper Jurassic time, and to some extent, robbed the original Eocene channel deposits and redeposited their gold.

The Yuba River placer gold deposit was formed when the present day Yuba River dissected the ancient Tertiary River channels and transported and reconcentrated the gold of the old river gravels. In addition to the gold deposited by natural geologic processes, the upper portion of the original deposit consisted of old tailings from hydraulic mines operated further upstream during the last half of the 19th century. These tailings were low grade and ranged in depth from about 45 feet on the fringes of the field to about 100 feet on the upstream or east portion of the field.

The high-grade gravel occurs in streaks throughout the deposit. Most of these streaks are in the lower portion of the deposit near bedrock. The bedrock under the pay gravel is the typical volcanic tuff of the Sierras, altered and consolidated in some places, and usually contains no gold. The last true bedrock is greenstone, which crops out near the river at Daguerra Point.

The highest grade portion of the deposit was the east or upstream portion nearest the mouth of the canyon. From here the grade decreased and the pay streaks became deeper toward the southwest or downstream portion of the field. Little if any dredgable ground is believed to exist west of the present downstream boundary of the field.

Most of the field has been dredged at least twice, although some of the virgin ground exists in the southwest part of the field. Some parts of the field have been dredged three or four times, each time to a greater depth with more efficient recovery equipment. Dredging conditions are good and the gravel is mostly medium-to-fine in particle size with few large boulders. The gravel includes cobbles and pebbles of gabbro, diorite and quartz. □

Yuba Dredge No. 21
This is a "working" operation and is on private property. It is not open to the public with traffic stopped at a Security building. The dredge is below the level of the surrounding ground, is some distance from the public road, and is not within sight of the highway.　　—Editor

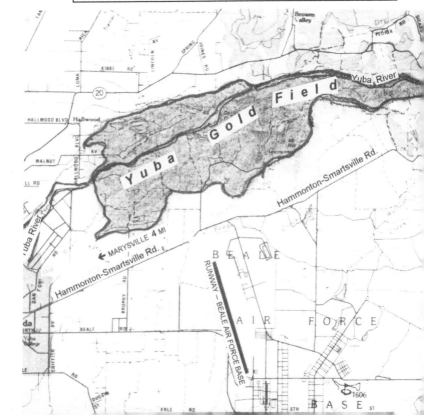

DREDGE No. 21 SPECIFICATIONS

Construction design	Yuba
Estimated annual capacity	4.1 million cu.yd.
Estimated annual production (92% fine)	20,000 - 25,000 ounces
Hull length	223 feet
Hull width	68 feet
Hull depth	11½ feet
Height of rear gantry	101 feet
Length of bow gantry	91 feet
Bucket size	20 cubic feet
Number of buckets	140-142
Bucket speed	0-27 buckets per minute
Length of ladder	230 feet
Weight of ladder with buckets	730 tons
Ladder suspended by 28 parts of 1¾" wire rope	
Digging depth (below water level)	140 feet
Length of main stacker	225 feet
Length of swing stacker	52 feet
Overall dredge length (level)	453 feet
Overall dredge weight	3,800 tons
5 water pumps - total	17,900 GPM
6 sand pumps - total	12,520 GPM
Approximate concentrated horsepower including:	2,700 HP
2 each 400 HP D.C. variable speed motors for bucketline drive	
High tension line voltage	60,000/4160V
Dredge voltage	460V
Washing screen (trommel)	9' diameter x 50½' long

Jigs:

Rougher -	48 cells being	42" x 42"
Cleaner:	8 cells being	42" x 42"
2nd Cleaner -	2 cells being	24" x 24"
3rd Cleaner -	2 cells being	12" x 12"

Operation scheduled 24 hours per day

Employees:

Dredge	24
Shops	16
Conveyor	1
Recovery	5
Warehouse	1
Administration	7
Total	54

Natroma Dredge No. 7 was wrecked in spring 1916. Top: Photo of wreck on April 20. Then, on May 27th, with cables attached, the dredge, having been mostly pumped out, was refloated with a splash.

Nat #7
Mar. 20-16

Nat #7
May 27 1916
7-70

NAT #7
May 27 19.
7-71

Chapter 5.

Trouble

In maritime circles it has been said:

The way to ruin a perfectly nice day is to wreck your ship.

What about a wrecked dredge or two?

Throughout the history of the dredgers, we find several mentions, and even photographs, of wrecked dredges. There appears to be at least two major reason why a dredge would sink.

1. When dredges were operating in rivers, severe spring floods could cause havoc with a moored dredge. The wire rope used to tie (moor) the dredge in place on shore would hopefully hold while the flood waters rose. But, if one set of lines on, say, the starboard side snapped or the stakes on the bank pull out – let go – while the port side lines held, as the water rose the tied-down side of the dredge stayed fairly level while the opposite side rose with the flood eventually toppling the dredge onto its port side.

2. It was considered to be real trouble when there was a break in the bucket chain. All the weight of the buckets and ladder crashing to the bottom of the river or pond upended the dredge leaving the stern and stacker high in the air. In the process, the bucket chain succeeded in becoming tangled. If lower deck hatches (the super-structure was often four or five stories tall) were not closed – they usually were not closed – water could rush in and sink the dredge.

The Liberty Dredge was digging in the bottom of its pond when the bank of earth immediately in front of it collapsed causing a sudden giant wave in the pond that raised the front of the dredge. As the pond settled, it piled the dredge on top of a very large underwater snag that punched a hole in the hull. This caused the dredge to sink. It took about one week to pump out the pond,

Tangle of buckets from an early wreck on Yuba Dredge No. 2 in Sacramento Valley.

clean the dredge's interior, repair the hull then refill the pond, before the dredge could be refloated so it could resume work.

The items needing replacement the most were the lips of the buckets. Most buckets were made of cast-iron but the removable lips were often manganese steel. It was the bucket lips that took the beating because of the constant striking against rocks on the river or pool's bottom.

Another place of concern were the pins in the linking that held the buckets to the chain. The only so-called lubrication these received was the water of the pond as it was believed that any grease in the pond was detrimental to the gold recovery process. Sometimes the pins that held the buckets to the chain broke because of wear-and-tear. These pins, for a dredge with 8 cu. ft. buckets, weigh 197 pounds each and were 5½-inches in diameter. A bucket of this size weighed between 2,300 and 2,600 pounds. To pull a broken pin and hoist the bucket to free the pin, took

Bucket pin from Yankee Fork Dredge. It weighs 197 pounds.

block-and-tackle with several men. When a pin was noted to be wearing, maintenance crews tried to make pin changes on the shut-down work day.

A well-engineered dredge was built to "balance" due to the overhanging weight of the bucket ladder on the bow and the long, heavy stacker sticking out from the stern. Many of the dredgers had wire-rope over the roofs tying the two gantries together as a safety measure to avoid upsets if either gantry fell. The earliest dredgers lacked this guy rope, as did Sumpter No. 3 which was built in 1935 thus it was not "early." (Old No. 1 had the ropes.)

In one instance at Sumpter, No. 3 dredge had a malfunction

71

THIS DREIGE #8 AFTER WATER WAS PUMP OUT TAKEN BY GUY FISHER. GUY JORGENSON WAS

Wreck of Natroma No. 8 after water was pumped out and ready for righting.

while the operator was trying to lift the spud which was very well stuck in the mud. While applying additional power, the strain caused the stacker to crash. During the emergency repairs, the two gantries were finally lashed together with wire-rope to avoid a reoccurrence.

On later dredges, as the Bucyrus-Erie at Yankee Fork, constructed in 1940 (Chapter 3), the internal steel construction eliminated the need for the guy-ropes.

Because the dredges usually shut down one day each week for cleanup, gold amalgam extraction and repairs, lip replacement was done at this time unless there had been some emergency break during the week that caused an immediate shut-down.

Many of the newer dredges had automatic graph-printers built on a 24-hour clock. The printers recorded the depth at which the buckets were digging, the time-of-day, and shut-downs. See the photographs in Chapter 3. □

Chapter 6.
Doodle-bugs and Other Dredges

"Doodle-bugs" were common where ever there was placer mining possibilities. Several of these toy-size (when compared to the mammoth Yuba and Bucyrus dredgers, were set up in the Sumpter Valley. Two of the operations were the Northwest Development Company and the Consuelo Oregon Mines. But Bucyrus also built dragline dredges. The name for this model was "Bucyrus Monicker."

While the larger Yuba-type dredges were "self-contained," most of the doodle-bugs were made up of two or three free-standing sections. The gravel-washing gold-separating plant was in a shed-like building that was set up off the ground about as tall as a two-story building. There was a crane with a drag-line" that scooped up the gravel then dumped it into the hopper on top of the gravel-washing unit. The third piece, if the particular outfit had such, was a second crane. This machine also used a drag-line just to scrape off then dump the top soil out of the way exposing the gold-bearing gravel for the other dragline to dig into.

A major exception to the rule was the doodler on Cracker Creek run by Max Hoffman. In reality, it looked more like a miniature Yuba for it did its own digging and had a small stacker appropriate to the size of the dredge.

Some of the doodle-bugs were diesel powered, others, if near power, used electricity. The Monighan at Sumpter was electrified. ("Monighan" was apparently a manufacturer's name.) An electric operation was much preferred as it meant a cleaner operation, less breakdown, and no fuel oil hauling and storage troubles such as spills. A diesel-powered doodle-bug took extra manpower, added to expenses, and interrupted the main work of digging for gold due to usual troubles with internal combustion engines.

The doodle-bug Bucyrus Monicker in the John Day Valley in the 1930's.

The doodle-bugs could work in areas where the Yuba's would not fit due to their much smaller size. Sumpter No. 2, a Yuba, had to quit near Bourne on Cracker Creek when it ran out of space in which to work. But Hoffman's doodlebug operation got in there and moved right along. (This was not the only time that Sumpter No. 2 ran out of work. The experience is recounted in the chapter "Liberty Dredge on Swauk Creek.")

In Eastern Oregon there were doodlebugs on Dixie Creek at Prarie City and some worked the John Day River up from the City of John Day, and nearby creeks, between Prairie City and Mt. Vernon, to mention only a few.

All doodle-bug operators did not meet with success. Among the various reasons was the obviously smaller size single bucket on the dragline when compared with the heavy chain of considerably larger buckets on a Yuba. The little dredgers did not have the power or the weight to successfully dig in very hard and rocky ground. But in the right place, a doodle-bug operation paid very well. One of the money-makers was Bill Dobbyn's outfit working on Jackson Creek right in the City of Jacksonville in Western Oregon. He had to quit when the dredge reached the concrete North Oregon Street Bridge. Bill told the author he is sorry now

Was a Doodle-Bug Operation Profitable?

Bill Dobbyn and Fred Christean had formed a partnership doing business as C. & D. Mining Company. On April 22, 1946, the United States Mint issued a BULLION DEPOSIT—MEMO REPORT in the favor of the partnership. The report relates to gold the men recovered from Jackson Creek for the preceeding week. For their week's work, the men split $1,217.48 between them.

Weight of the bar of raw gold on receipt		40.97 oz.
Weight after melt		39.85 oz.
Assay Certificateof Fineness:		
Gold		874¾
Silver		111
Base		014¼
Value:		
Gold @ $34.858		$1,220.03
Silver $ .70		$ 3.09
Administrative Costs:		
Melting	1.00	
Refining	1.59	
Handling	3.05	
TOTAL CHARGES	**5.64**	
NET VALAUE (AFTER COSTS)		$1,217.48

that during the period – right after World War II – he, and his partner Fred Chrtistean, were too busy hauling out gold to think of making any pictures. ☐

When an operator quit dredging, the dredge was often abandoned and left to rot. This remains was near Folsom on American River.

75

With mining stopped, this Yuba dredge at Callahan, California was partially dismantled with ladder and stacker put on the ground, to lesson the strain on the gantries, years ago. Photo made in 1971 by Bert Webber. The dredge was recently sold, further taken apart then was shipped to Bolivia. LOWER: This dredge waddled down the John Day River from that city, was stopped by a concrete highway bridge at Mt. Vernon when officials would not allow the bridge be dismantled for the pleasure of the miners.

Empire Dredge No. 1 in 1901, worked in the John Day country of Eastern Oregon. This may be same dredge shown years later at bottom of page 76. LOWER: Only known working model of Yuba dredge is Natroma No. 10 in Folsom Historical Museum, Folsom, California.

Empire Dredge No. 2 on June 17, 1916 during construction. CENTER: Empire No. 2 worked in the Canyon City - John Day area for years. LOWER: Empire No. 2 on July 12, 1916 at John Day.

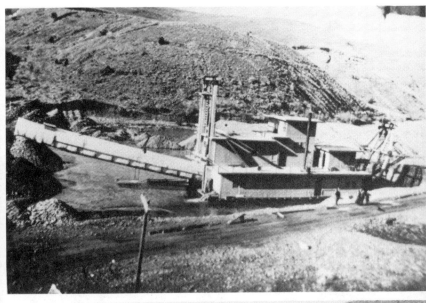

Unidentified dredge in the Yuba Gold Field. Note water flowing back into pond. Early-day recycling? Paddock dredging did not depend on fresh-flowing water to operate. When the dredge moved, it took its water, and its pond, with it. LOWER: British built dredge , *ca* 1904, in a river in Siberia.

Yuba dredge working Foots Creek in Jackson County, Oregon in 1941.

Dredging on Foots Creek

Foots Creek rises in the foothills of Mt. Isabella and flows rapidly downhill entering the Rogue River a little east of the town of the same name in Jackson County, Oregon. Records indicate dredging was started in the creek about 1903 by the Champlin Electric Gold Dredging Company. This mining venture started with steam power but when the Gold Ray Dam, on the river, opened in 1905, a line was run for the use of the dredger.

The Yuba-type dredge had 36, 8 cu. ft. buckets on its ladder and could handle about 2,000 yards a day. In 1911 some kind of accident befell the dredge which caused a temporary shut down of the mining. Nosik wrote that a replacement dredge was brought in and some parts from the wreck were salvaged. But other parts were abandoned to be eventually covered by forest duff and mud.

In 1978, Robert Nosik discovered three of the buckets that

Very few dredges were built with twin stackers. TOP: Early steam powered model. LOWER: Electric dredger in Sacramento Valley. There is at least one instance when a contract was made with the Corps of Engineers for a twin-stacker to dump gravel to Corps specifications to build levees on both side of a river in one sweep.

over the years had become buried. He dug them up. A local senior citizen gentleman, when interviewed, recalled that decades earlier he and a friend had played on the broken dredge. How was the dredge damaged?

Other dredgers operated on both forks of Foots Creek until about 1935 when work stopped. Finally, parts for still another dredge came to the creek in 1939 and just weeks later the dredger was working. It was now the Murphy Murray Dredging Company. This dredge, electrically operated, was on a barge 81-feet long and 37-feet wide. It was fully equipped with a ladder that sup-ported 67 buckets of 3½ cu. ft. capacity each and dug to a depth of 20 feet. It could feed 4,000 yards a day into its screening and washing system and kick out gravel from its stacker. In the spring of 1941, apparently at the end of its land holdings, the dredge was dismantled and moved. □

LOWER right: Weekend prospectors mostly pan for gold but today many serious gold-diggers use (TOP): gasoline powered *KEENE* floating portable dredges. Venture suction action moves up to 1,500 gallons per min., will awaken nearby residents at dawn. Triple sluice recovery systems catch even fine gold. Powered by Briggs, Honda or Volkswagen engines, for amateur or professional miners trying to find "color" in less time.

This two-man operation was spotted near Liberty, Washington on July 16, 1994. Left man operates vacuum hose to pick up gravel and sand from creek's bottom. Right man shovels sand into hopper. These prospectors were so intent the cameraman was never observed.

83

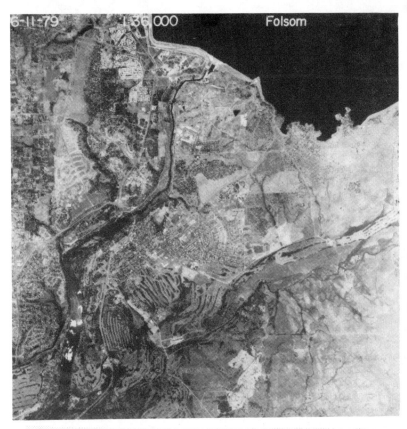

U.S. Army Corps of Engineers aerial photograph of Folsom, California, shows reservoir (top right corner); American River flowing from dam; town and line-after-line-after-line of tailings. All but historic part of town built on tailings. LOWER: Area near American River leveled, sewers in, ready for construction of expensive homes.

Chapter 7.
Tailings – Mountains of Gravel!

To hear some folks talk, the worst catastrophe to occur in placer mining areas are the mountains of gravel – rocks – that are spewed out the back end of dredges as dredgers dig up river bottoms and ponds searching for gold. It is not our mission here to debate the environmental issues posed by these almost endless, in some areas, mountains or gravel.

We have made some observations based on what is in the literature, newspapers, magazines and books.

Weatherbe, writing in 1917, in his *Dredging For Gold in California*, devotes a chapter to "The Horticultural Question."

In the Oroville Tract covering as much as 6,000 acres, he points out that less than 400 acres had been planted in fruit but most of the land was of very poor quality and was without irrigation. Of the 400 acres planted, about 150 were in a vineyard infested with *phylloxera*. A peach orchard [produced only one "average" crop in three years and might provide an income of 6% on $100 per acre. Many acres were valued at about $50 each with a total value on the tract of about $250,000. Weatherbe pointed out:

It is a well known fact that most of the ranches in this district were mortgaged. If we say the district will yield on average 10¢ per yard net profit and averages eight yards in depth, both fairly conservative estimates, then over $23,000,000 in net profits will be produced, and if invested at 6%, will preduce an annual income of over $1,380.000 instead of the paltry revenue of only $15,000 per year which this land produced before. Further, for a long period, a large population will be employed and at the end of the period of operation, another $20,000,000 should have been expended in labor and machinery.

Experimental planting of
Eucalyptus trees about 1915 in
Sacramento Valley tailings.

RIGHT PAGE → Eucalyptus and other trees in "the grove," planted
decades ago in the rocks at Folsom as photographed in July 1994.

In the Folsom area he found similarities between returns from
crops verses value of the same land for dredge mining. He mentions the Natroma Vinyards & Winery Company and the
population is supported in its agriculture and winery operations.
He found there were many "busybodies" and "other uninterested
parties" that attempted by "unwarranted agitation" to cause
trouble.

Weatherbe was interested in seeing if dredged land – tailings
– could be put into agriculture. He wrote:

> After dredging, the land is covered with stack piles containing boulders
> and pebbles the fine material being hidden 6 to 15 feet below. Certain
> experiments carried out by Mr. J. H. Leggett, at Oroville, produced interesting
> results. Eucalyptus of both the "blue" and "red-gum" varieties and some fig
> trees were planted in stack piles (tailings) and alfalfa grass is also growing.
> The trees when set out were only about 10-inches high.

After two years, the Eucalyptus trees were 19 feet tall. He
said that some of the trees were planted on the very top of the
highest rock piles, about 15 feet higher than the surrounding land.

Weatherbe pointed out that in Leggett's experiments

Mason Dam on the Powder River in Baker County, near Sumpter, Oregon was built with tons of tailings from the Sumpter dredges. There is no shortage of tailings for other projects needing land fill, railroad ballast, rocks, gravel for mixing with cement, or even for building monuments.

Example of tailings being blown out of stacker with compressed air. This technique caused the gravel to be spewed farther away from the edge of the pile, minimizing fall-back into the pond.

...one cannot dig a hole at any of these highest points more than 2 feet without getting moisture even in the driest time of summer. The volcanic ash forms the bottom of the digging and the material of certain clay bands is often carried over the stacker in lumps and disintegrates on being exposed to the air so as to form the soil necessary for growth. The alfalfa roots were accidentally thrown up by the dredge and seems to be doing particularly well. Absolutely no care was given to the trees or alfalfa from the time they were set out.

Near Oroville, the original land owner of a tract that was dredged agreed to put the ground in a suitable state for cultivation if it was given to him. He leveled one acre and covered it with one foot of top spoil and now has a productive garden. His costs for leveling and covering being $250.

Weatherbe cited there were good examples of use at Folsom where the tailings "are to become a valuable asset." He pointed out that a rock crusher was in use to make ballast (small rocks) for use by railroads, highways and for concrete.

In Oregon, the Mason Dam, on the Powder River, built 1966-1968, consumed load after load after load of tailings left from the Sumpter dredges.

In Folsom, the only area specifically studied for this book for use of tailings, the fact that these mountains of gravel exist does not seem to bother any of the developers, as the photographs illustrate. □

Bulldozer levels mounds of tailings readying the rocks for a building contractor. Photographed at Folsom on July 5, 1994. LOWER: Lemby Athletic Park, built on a leveled rock pile, uses more rocks to support its display sign.

At Folsom, entire real estate development projects are built on tailings and nobody seems to mind. If one is handed lemons, make lemonade. If its rocks, build with or on them. Want green grass? Buy ready-grown sod.

APPENDIX 1
Powder River Gold Dredging Company
(California Corporation)
Sumpter District
Baker County, Oregon

The Mineral Resources of Oregon - Oregon Bureau of Mines and Geology December 1916

The most important placer mining operation in the state is that of the Powder river Gold Dredging Company located near Sumpter, Oregon. The total; holdings of the company is about 2,500 acres of which about 700 acres are to be dredged. This 700 acres of commercial gravel extends from a point a short distance south of Sumpter to McEwan, a total distance of about 5 miles

The commercial gravel is in a meandering channel from 300 to 2,00 feet wide and averaging about 1,000 feet, and occupies only a part of the valley floor. The average depth of the gravel is about 18 to 20 feet. The bedrock is a soft decomposed rock with dredge men call "clay webfoot." Nearly all of the gold is on bedrock and the condition of the gravel and bedrock is such as to be called quite hard digging. This fact will be better understood when it is known that the manganese steel bucket lips last only 5 months while in California practice they last about 18 months.

The two dredges are of the standard type and were constructed by the Yuba Construction Company of Marysville, Cal. On Dredge No. 1, the 65 buckets have a capacity of 9 cubic feet each and on No. 2 dredge 7½ cubic feet each and the dredges will dig to a maximum depth of 30 feet.

The two dredges have an actual capacity of about 10,000 cubic yards daily. The dredges have wood hulls, which, according to California experience, have an average life of 10 to 12 years. They have no amalgamating plates. They are equipped with Hungarian riffles which have a slope of 1¼ inches to a foot of length.

The power is furnished by the Eastern Oregon Light and Power Company. The horsepower required is naturally variable. The consumption averages about 750 HP in 7 motors for each dredge.

The clean-up is made weekly and the night extraction, estimated at 95 percent, is made upon easily washed gravels which contain but little clay. The gold is medium course. The particles average larger than those in the California dredging field. The largest nugget secured is 5-eights by 3-eights inch while perforations in the revolting screen are three-fourths inch. It is evident that no nuggets of gold are lost in the oversize. The average fineness of the gold is 785. The total cost per yard is approximately 3½¢ which is higher than California practice due largely to the more difficult diggings.

Between 100 and 105 acres were dredged from February 1, 1913 to October 8, 1914, a period of about 20 months, or about 60 acres annually.

This was done with Dredge No. 1.

The company secured in November 1914 some additional ground for which negotiations had been in progress for some time. Since this purchase has been effected, they began in spring of 1915 the digging of a pit to install another dredge to work the ground upstream from the point where the present dredge began to dredge the channel downstream toward McEwan. This boat was completed in October 1915 and has been operated steadily ever since then with gratifying results. □

Oregon Metal Mines Handbook Department of Geology and Mineral Industries State of Oregon
Bulletin 14-A. 1939

Sumpter Valley Dredging Company, an Oregon Corporation

Located about 5 miles below Sumpter in Sumpter Valley.

Area: About 1,100 acres, began operations June 25. 1935 with probable life of 8 additional years from January 1, 1939.

Ground has been entirely drilled with values to 60 feet deep; no deeper drilling done but gravel does go deeper; digging 13 to 16 feet to false clay bedrock. Very few boulders, mainly size of football and smaller. Gold fineness, 800. Average yardage handles for year 1938 was 280,000 cubic yards per month, or about 10 acres.

Equipment consists of a boat hull, 52 feet by 120 feet by 11 feet; stacker, 96 feet with 36 inch belt.

Bucket line has 72 buckets of 9 cubic feet capacity each dumping at rate of 25-per-minute.

Trommel screen 6 feet by 36 feet, 4,200 square feet of tables with save-all full length of the dredge.

Power: Electric, supplied by 12 mile 23,000 volt line to portable substation, stepped drown to 2,300 volts for boat, 710 HP connected load with 1,250 HP on digging line There are two 10 inch pumps and one 6 inch pump supplying 8,000 gallons of water per minute.

Refining: Amalgam is retorted and melted at plant and bricks of gold shipped to U.S. Assay Office in Seattle, Washington.

Other equipment includes an office, sand house, machine shops, two No. 40 diesel tractors and two trucks.

General matters: 23 men are employed with annual payroll of $50,000 to $60,000. Power cost: About $30,000. Machine shop and additional supplies, about $60,000. Taxes and other general operating costs about $15,000. □

APPENDIX 2
How many Dredges are There and Where Are They?
➔ **Dredging for Gold was not limited to the United States**

Extent of British Owned Gold Dredging Operations in 1904
Number of Dredges in Each Company Not Stated
(Source: *The Mining Journal* - London)

Argentina - 1 company
Bolivia - 1 company
Canada (British Columbia) - 11 companies
Chili, 1 company
Columbia, 5 companies
Dutch Guinea - company
French Guinea - 1 company
Gold Coast - Africa - 10 companies
Malay Peninsula - 2 company
Mozambique, Africa - 6 companies
New Zealand - 3 companies
Patagonia - 1 company
Peru - 1 company
Rhodesia, Africa, 3 companies
Russia, 2 company
Serbia, 1 company
Siberia - 1 company
Spain - 2 company
United States - Yuba County, California 3 companies
Yukon River, Alaska - 1 company

Operations in California
Statement of D'Arcy Weatherby
Mining and Scientific Press. 1904.

Oroville, Yuba, Folsom fields: 49 dredges

Statement by Peggy Bal (1979)
Dredging on the Yuba River Goldfields Site hold the record for the longest continuous placer mining operation (1905-1968)* in the world. During the period, 21 dredges were used. When the operations reached the town of Hammonton, the buildings were sold, moved, then the townsite was dredged.

* Although there was a period of inactivity, Yuba Dredge No. 21, rebuilt and enlarged, is operating in 1994. —Editor

APPENDIX 3
Transportabilityof Dredges in the Field....

Transportability of dredges in the field away from waterways in California

The means of transport was to disassemble a dredge then pack it to a new site on the backs of mules. Data here is for a 3½-cu. ft. Bucyrus dredge and the divisibility of its parts: Approximate weight of intact dredge: 196,400 lbs.
Upper tumbler, 6,500 lbs
Cut into 20 pieces one at 1,000 lbs each other less than 300 lbs.
Lower tumbler, 4,500 lbs.
Cuts into 13 pieces, three at about 700 lbs. the rest about 300 lbs.
Digging ladder, 28,000 lbs.
Dismantles to 2 pieces of 600 lbs, the rest at about 300 lbs.
Digging buckets (3½ ft.)
Bottom about 320 lbs., each hood 135 lbs. each lip 120 lbs.
Screen, stacker and parts, 16,000 lbs.
8 pieces about 600 lbs each, other parts 350 lbs, nearly 60% less than 300 lbs.
Gears, 30,000 lbs.
8 parts about 700 lbs each, other parts 350 lbs, nearly 50% less than 300 lbs.
Engine or motors 15,000 lbs.
2 pieces about 1,000 lbs.; 2 pieces about 600 lbs.; nearly 50% below 350 lbs.
Boilers, 8,500 lbs.
All below 350 lbs.
Winches, 42,000 lbs.
2 pieces 600 lbs., other pieces below 350 lbs.
Pumps, 300 lbs.
2 pieces each 150 lbs.
Other parts, 7,600 lbs.
All pieces under 350 lbs.
—Source: D'Arcy Weatherbe in *Mining and Scientific Press* San Francisco. Nov. 17, 1906.

About the Author

Bert Webber is a Research Photojournalist who likes to look for subjects that have not been earlier presented in books or, if there has been such a book, he is able to find material that would make for a better one. His subjects are all non-fiction, are mostly about Oregon and the Oregon Trail and some unique matters of World War II in the Pacific. These books are aimed for use by librarians as source material, are usually loaded with pictures, and all are written at *Reader's Digest* level for popular readability.

Webber graduated from Whitworth College in Journalism and in Library Science. Later, he earned the Master of Library Science by studying at Portland State University and the University of Portland. He was a teacher and school librarian but retired from that profession in 1970 to pursue full-time writing.

Bert Webber has hundreds of newspaper and magazine articles and over forty books. He is listed in *Who's Who in the West, Who's Who in the World* and in *Contemporary Authors.* For a hobby, he plays baritone horn in the Southern Oregon Symphonic Band where he also serves on the band's Board of Control.

Bert and his wife, Margie, a retired Registered Nurse, who is co-author of some of the books, have four grown children and eight grandchildren. They live in Oregon's Rogue River Valley just a few miles from where Bill Dobbyn ran his doodle-bug. □

Bibliography

Bal, Peggy. *Pebbles in the Stream; A History of Beale Air Force Base and Neighboring Areas.* Easter Publishing Co. (Chico, Calif.). 1979.

Brooks, Howard C and Len Ramp. *Gold and Silver in Oregon.* [Bulletin 61 Department of Geology and Mineral Industries - State of Oregon]. 1968.

Cockle, Dick. Ðredging Up Memories" in *Oregon Magazine.* V. 13. No. 6. p.11. June/July 1983.

Castaneda, Antonia [*et al.*] *Natromas Company 1851-1984.* (unprinted ms.) 1984. (Folsom Historical Society)

Engineers' Reports Show the Kittitas Gold Mining Company Property. (Investment Prospectus) Kittitas Gold Mining Company (Ellensburg, Wash.) n.d. [*ca* 1925].

Hansen, Harry, Ed. *California, A Guide to the Golden State.* [Federal Writer's Project]. Hastings. 1939.

Jennings, Hennen. *The History and Development of Gold Dredging in Montana.* Dept. of the Interior. Bulletin No, 121. US Gov Print Office. 1916.

Jordan, Josee. *You're at Liberty Here.* Private Print. 1967.

Lemert, Ann Arnold. *First You Take A Pick & A Shovel.* The John Bradford Press. 1979.

Longridge, C. C. *Gold Dredging.* [London] *The Mining Journal.* 1905.

Nosik, Lillian Knotek. "A Historical Review of Gold Dredging on Foots Creek" in *Southern Oregon Sunrise.* July 1978 pp. 34-36.

Oliver, Herman. *Gold and Cattle Country.* Binford and Mort. 1961.

Packard, Howard A. Jr. *Gold Dredge on the Yankee Fork.* [Private Print]. 1983.

"Reader Asks For History of Gold Dredging Operations in the Yuba [River]." in *Advocate-Democrat.* Yuba City [Calif.]. Jun 22, 1994.

Stahlberg, John A. *Montana; A State Guide Book.* [Federal Writer's Project] Viking. 1939.

Sumpter Valley Dredge State Park, Final Draft - Master Plan. Oregon Parks and Recreation Dept. 1994.

Wagner, Jack R. *Gold Mines of California.* Howell-North. n.d.

Custer, A Walking Guide of Custer, Idaho. Fr. of Custer Museum (Inc.). n.d.

Weatherby, D'Arcy. *Dredging For Gold in California.* Mining and Scientific Press (San Francisco). 1917.

Walling, A. G. *History of Southern Oregon....* Walling Co., 1884.

Webber, Bert and Margie. *Jacksonville, Oregon; The Making of a National Historic Landmark.* YeGalleon. 1982.

Illustration Credits

Index

Photographs and maps are indicated by *bold italic* page numbers

99